The Little Witch's Black Magic Cookbook

The Little Witch's Black Magic Cookbook

by Linda Glovach

PRENTICE-HALL, INC.
Englewood Cliffs, N.J.

for Ellen and Kate

The Little Witch's Black Magic Cookbook
by Linda Glovach
Copyright © 1972 by Linda Glovach
All rights reserved. No part of this book may be
reproduced in any form or by any means, except
for the inclusion of brief quotations in a review,
without permission in writing from the publisher.
Printed in the United States of America
Prentice-Hall International, Inc., London
Prentice-Hall of Australia, Pty. Ltd., North Sydney
Prentice-Hall of Canada, Ltd., Toronto
Prentice-Hall of India Private Ltd., New Delhi
Prentice-Hall of Japan, Inc., Tokyo

Library of Congress Cataloging in Publication Data
Glovach, Linda.
The little witch's black magic cookbook.
SUMMARY: Easy recipes using inexpensive and easily
available ingredients. Also includes holiday ideas.
1. Cookery—Juvenile literature. [1. Cookery]
I. Title:
PZ10.G545Li   641.5   72-2111
ISBN 0-13-53760-5
ISBN 0-13-537936-9 p6k.

10   9   8   7   6   5

INTRODUCTION

This cookbook for little witches is also for boys. The recipes are easy and not very fancy, so don't worry if you make a mistake here and there. If the chicken should get soggy when you are making Chicken Cones, or if your Secret Spell Birthday Cakes topple over, that's all right. These are special little witch formulas and they will taste delicious anyway.

After you have read The Little Witch's Code a few times, you will be ready to start cooking. Be sure to keep a sponge handy in case you have to wipe up something in a hurry.

CONTENTS

Introduction / 5

I. The Little Witch's Code / 8
   Utensils / 10

II. Snacks / 13
   Frosted Funnies / 14
   Creamy Crunchies / 16
   Ghost Toast / 18

III. Brews & Potions / 19
   Chocolate Shivers / 20
   Grape Lemonaches / 21
   Ghost Floats / 22

IV. Lunches / 25
   Tangerine Dream Salad / 26
   Chicken Cones / 28
   Pickled Peanut Butter Burgers / 31

V. Holidays and Special Occasions / 33
   BIRTHDAYS / 34
   Secret Spell Birthday Cakes / 34

   VALENTINE'S DAY / 36
   Sweetheart Sandwiches / 36
   Valentine Tea Party / 36
   Ticklish Tea / 37

MOTHER'S DAY & FATHER'S DAY   /   38
Bewitching Breakfast in Bed   /   38
Cinnamon Toast   /   39

HALLOWEEN   /   40
Halloween Scream Party   /   40
Spooky Sprinkle Dip   /   42
Witch Mix-Up   /   43

CHRISTMAS
Cucumber Christmas Tree   /   44

VI. How to Make A Witch's Hat   /   45

  Index   /   48

I. THE LITTLE WITCH'S CODE

1. *Before* you start making anything, read your recipe carefully. Do this a few times to make sure you understand it.

2. Gather all the things you will need so you won't have to look for something with sticky hands in the middle of a recipe. Everything you need is listed at the top of the recipe.

3. If you think a recipe looks too hard for you to make alone, get someone to help you, like a big brother or a mother. This is especially true when you are using the blender.

4. The usual preparing time is listed with each recipe, so that you will know how long you'll need the kitchen. But don't use the kitchen until you have asked your mother and she says it's all right. Even little witches can get in the way sometimes.

5. Don't forget to clean up when you are finished. If any food is left over, put it away so that it will be there the next time you need it. Wash your dishes and don't forget to sweep the floor with your witch's broom.

6. Now if you think you understand everything, you can start cooking. Remember—wash your hands first and be sure to keep a sponge handy in case you have to wipe up something in a hurry.

UTENSILS

Knife

Large Plate

Fork

Small Plate

Large Bowl

Measuring Cup

Small Bowl

Measuring Spoons

Pitcher

Small Glasses

Stirring Spoon

Blender

Tall Glasses

Heart-Shaped Cookie Cutter

Toaster

Tray

Toothpicks

Teapot   Teacups

FROSTED FUNNIES

15 minutes
3 servings

SMALL BOWLS
MEASURING SPOONS
MEASURING CUP
FORK
KNIFE

½ cup confectioners sugar
1 teaspoon butter (soft) or shortening
1 tablespoon milk
food coloring
1 small box of animal crackers

Mix the sugar and the butter in a bowl with a fork.

Add the milk very slowly. Stir until it is very creamy.

Divide the frosting into 2 parts and put each part in a bowl. In each bowl add drops of food coloring to make the colors you like. Stir with a fork until the color is even.

Spread the frosting on the animal crackers with a knife, a little bit at a time.

CREAMY CRUNCHIES

10 minutes
2 or 3 servings

KNIFE
SMALL PLATE
MEASURING SPOONS

1 apple
3 tablespoons cream cheese
1 tablespoon strawberry jam

Cut the apple in half. Lay one half cut side down and slice it with a knife into four or five pieces the way the little witch is doing in the picture.

Do the same thing to the other half.

Cut out the core from each piece.

Spread each piece of apple with cream cheese as though it were a slice of bread. Spread a little jam on top of the cheese. This is just enough for two hungry people or three people who aren't too hungry.

GHOST TOAST

5 minutes
2 servings

TOASTER
SMALL PLATE
MEASURING SPOON
KNIFE

2 slices of bread
1 tablespoon butter
3 tablespoons coconut

Toast the two slices of bread. Then spread them with butter. Put the coconut on a plate, spread it around, and put the buttered toast face down in it.

If there is some coconut left on the plate after you have done this, sprinkle what's left over on the toast.

III. BREWS & POTIONS

CHOCOLATE SHIVERS

10 minutes
2 servings

GLASSES
MEASURING CUP
MEASURING SPOON
STIRRING SPOON

½ cup milk
2 tablespoons chocolate syrup
1 cup club soda

Mix the milk and the chocolate syrup in two glasses—¼ cup milk and 1 tablespoon of chocolate syrup in each glass. Add ½ cup of club soda to each glass very slowly. Watch out— it fizzes!

Chocolate Shivers is very good with ice cream. Chocolate is best, and banana is also very good. If you do add a scoop of ice cream, make sure that the glass is only half-full at first, or you'll make a terrible mess.

GRAPE LEMONACHES

5 minutes
4 servings

MEASURING CUP
PITCHER
GLASSES
STIRRING SPOON

1 cup lemonade
2 cups grape juice

Mix the lemonade with the grape juice in a pitcher. Add ice if you like.

GHOST FLOATS

20 minutes BLENDER
2 servings MEASURING SPOON
            MEASURING CUP
            GLASSES

1 cup prepared powdered milk
(fresh milk won't work)
1 teaspoon vanilla extract
1 cup diet soda

Ask your mother to get the blender out of the cupboard.

Put the milk and the vanilla in the blender. Slowly add the soda.

Blend at medium speed for two minutes. Pour into two glasses and put them in the freezer for ten minutes.

When you take the drink out of the freezer you will see the ghosts floating on top. This is a great drink for mother witches on diets because it has only 57 calories. And the little witches who are not on a diet can use regular soda.

IV. LUNCHES

TANGERINE DREAM SALAD

10 minutes
2 servings

SMALL PLATE
MEASURING CUP

1 tangerine
2 or 3 lettuce leaves
1 cup of yogurt (any fruit flavor)

Take the skin off the tangerine and break it into sections.

Put the lettuce leaves on a plate and make a circle of the tangerine sections on the bed of lettuce. Put the yogurt in the middle of the tangerine sections.

This is very delicious and a lot of fun to eat. You dip each tangerine section into the yogurt and then pop it in your mouth.

This makes a nice lunch with a glass of milk and some cookies.

CHICKEN CONES

15 minutes   MEASURING SPOON
2 servings   MEASURING CUP
                  STIRRING SPOON
                  SMALL BOWL

1 cup leftover or canned chicken
1 tablespoon mayonnaise
1 tablespoon sweet pickle relish
2 ice cream cones

Shred the chicken into small pieces in a bowl.

Add the mayonnaise and the pickle relish. Stir until they are thoroughly mixed.

Put half the mixture into each cone.

This makes a good lunch if you also have a glass of milk and a banana for desert.

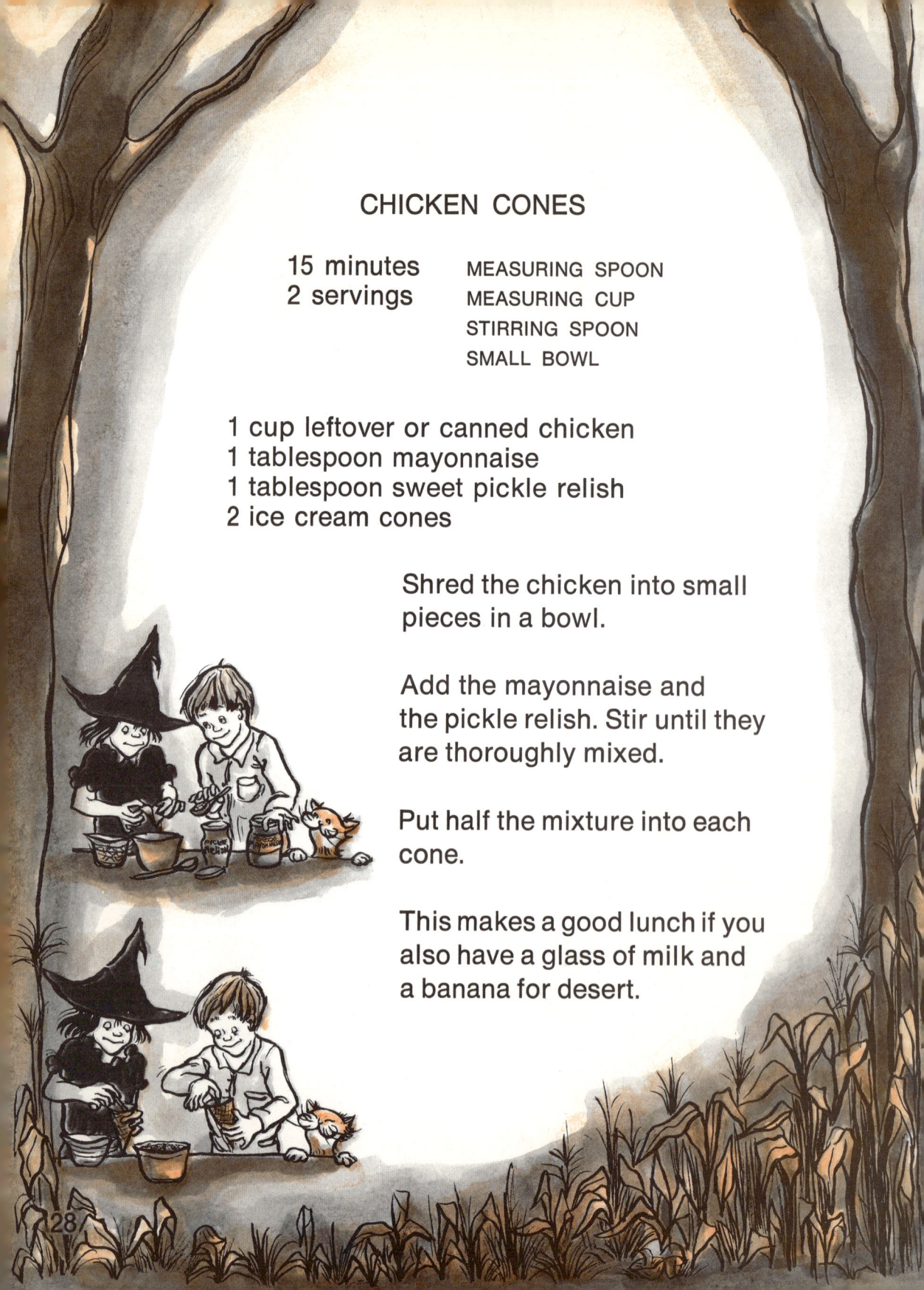

PICNIC LUNCH FOR TWO

If you live near a park or a field, you might have a picnic there sometime. You can also have a picnic in your backyard or on your front stoop. If you don't have a picnic basket, an empty shoe box is very handy. You can fit two apples, a thermos full of Grape Lemonaches (the recipe is on page 21) and two Pickled Peanut Butter Burgers into a shoe box.

PICKLED PEANUT BUTTER BURGERS

10 minutes   MEASURING SPOON
2 servings   KNIFE

2 hamburger rolls
1 tablespoon butter
4 tablespoons peanut butter
4 pickle slices (any kind you like)

Open the rolls and spread one side of each bun with butter.

Spread the other side with peanut butter.

Put two pickle slices on the peanut butter, and put the halves together.

Wrap them in waxed paper and put them in your picnic basket or shoe box.

 # BIRTHDAYS

The little witch is very fond of birthday cake, and so she makes Secret Spell Birthday Cakes when her grandmother or her best friend or anyone she likes has a birthday. This is a very good recipe because each person gets his own cake. Of course, only the birthday person gets candles on his cake.

SECRET SPELL BIRTHDAY CAKES

3 hours 20 minutes
6 servings

STIRRING SPOON
KNIFE
LARGE PLATE
MEASURING CUP

1 quart can whipped cream (whipped topping does not work)
24 chocolate wafers
food coloring
sprinkles

Squirt each cookie on one side with about a tablespoon of whipped cream. Then stack them in piles of four.

Put them in the freezer for at least three hours.

Just before serving, squirt ¾ cup of whipped cream into measuring cup. Add a few drops of food coloring and stir until the color is even. Try to pick a color that the birthday person likes.

Spread the colored whipped cream over the stacks of cookies so that you can't see the edges of the cookies. If you like, you can decorate the little cakes with sprinkles or maraschino cherries.

VALENTINE TEA PARTY

Next to Halloween, the little witch likes Valentine's Day best. She invites her dearest friends to tea, and they talk about their secret plans. Here are two of the little witch's special Valentine Day recipes:

SWEETHEART SANDWICHES

15 minutes
2 servings

KNIFE
HEART-SHAPED COOKIE CUTTER
PLATE

8 slices bread
2 tablespoons butter
2 tablespoons red jelly

Spread one side of each slice of bread with butter. Cut out a heart from each slice of bread with your cookie cutter.

36

Spread four of the heart shapes with jam or jelly. Make sandwiches of a slice with jelly and a slice with butter. Serve on a plate.

TICKLISH TEA

5 minutes
2 servings

MEASURING CUP
TEAPOT AND TEACUPS

1 cup ginger ale
1 cup orange juice

Pour the ginger ale and the orange juice into a teapot, or a pitcher if you don't have a teapot.

Stir a few times. You can add a few ice cubes if you like.

Serve in teacups and watch your friend giggle when the bubbles burst in his nose.

MOTHER'S DAY & FATHER'S DAY

Sometimes it is very hard to decide what to give your mother or father for their birthdays, or for Mother's Day and Father's Day. Something they will like very much is a surprise breakfast in bed. If it is your mother's birthday, be sure to tell your father what you are going to do. If it is Father's Day, tell your mother what you are going to do so that she can make sure that your father stays in bed until it is time.

BEWITCHING BREAKFAST IN BED

15 minutes
1 serving

GLASS   MEASURING SPOON
TOASTER   TRAY
KNIFE   PLATE

ORANGE JUICE
CINNAMON TOAST

2 slices bread
1 tablespoon butter
1 tablespoon sugar
1 teaspoon cinnamon

First pour the orange juice into a glass and put it on the tray. A vase of flowers or a cheerful card is nice to add to the tray.

Toast the bread. Spread the butter on it. Sprinkle sugar from a spoon over the buttered toast.

Now sprinkle the cinnamon (not too much!) so that it just covers the sugar.

HALLOWEEN SCREAM PARTY

October 31 is Halloween, a very special holiday for little witches. It is a time for celebrations and sweet treats. Why not ask your friends to come over to your house for a Halloween party? Tell them to wear costumes or to come just as they are.

Orange and black balloons and spooky crepe paper streamers turn a plain room into a witch's wonderland. A pitcher of Grape Lemonaches (the recipe is on page 21) is good to serve, and on the next page you will see some things you can make yourself for the party.

SPOOKY SPRINKLE DIP

10 minutes
for 8 people

SPOON
LARGE BOWL
LARGE PLATE

24 cookies, in different shapes and colors
1 cup of whipped cream or whipped topping
assorted sprinkles and red hots

Put the whipped cream or whipped topping in a bowl. Sprinkle the cream with red hots and colored sprinkles. Place the bowl on a plate and arrange the cookies around it.

Tell your guests to dip in—it's good! Spooky Sprinkle Dip is also very good with apple slices and licorice sticks.

WITCH MIX-UP

5 minutes
for 8 people

LARGE BOWL

1 cup popcorn or Cracker Jacks
½ cup candy corn
½ cup small marshmallows
½ cup black jelly beans or licorice dots

Mix all the ingredients together and serve in a pretty bowl.

CUCUMBER CHRISTMAS TREE

20 minutes

TOOTHPICKS
KNIFE
SMALL PLATE

1 cucumber
1 cup gumdrops of different colors
½ cup miniature marshmallows
one 12 inch strand red licorice rope

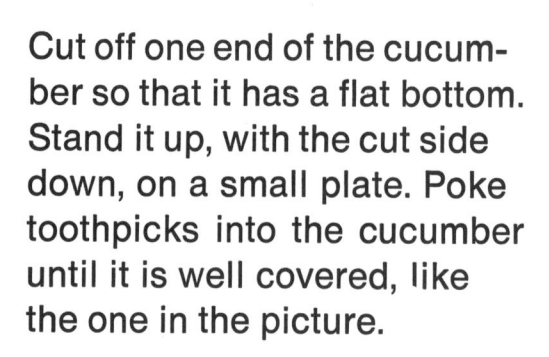

Cut off one end of the cucumber so that it has a flat bottom. Stand it up, with the cut side down, on a small plate. Poke toothpicks into the cucumber until it is well covered, like the one in the picture.

Now stick the gumdrops and the marshmallows on the toothpicks, the way the little witch is doing here.

String the red licorice over the toothpicks. This makes a great centerpiece, and a wonderful Christmas present for a friend who likes candy.

Merry Christmas

HOW TO MAKE A WITCH'S HAT

1 sheet black construction paper
      (12 inches long and 18 inches wide)
1 paper plate (8 inches diameter)
black crayon   Scotch tape
tape measure   stapler
scissors   pencil

Measure around your head with the tape measure. Add one inch to that measurement. Cut the sheet of construction paper so that it is that width. If your head measures 13 inches, add one inch to make it 14. Cut off 4 inches from the width of the construction paper to make it 14 inches.

Find the halfway point in the width of the paper. If it is 14 inches after you cut it, the halfway point will be 7 inches from each edge. Mark a dot at the top of the paper, the way the little witch is doing in the picture.

From the dot, draw diagonal lines to each side of the paper, ¾ of the way down the side.

Connect the diagonal lines along the width of the paper, with a curve that touches the bottom of the paper in the middle. Cut along the lines to remove excess paper.

Bring the edges together until they touch and overlap about ½ inch. Staple at the top and bottom. Seal the seam with Scotch tape. Now you have the crown of the witch's hat.

Rest the crown on the paper plate. With a pencil draw a line around it. Cut inside the line so that the brim is a tiny bit smaller than the crown. Color the paper plate brim black.

Slip the plate over the crown and leave 2 inches of the crown hanging out below the plate.

Slit the paper to make flaps to attach to the underneath part of the plate. Slit the paper in three places, each slit one inch deep.

Bend the flaps and fasten them to the brim with a stapler. If the paper crinkles, make the slits a little longer. Now smooth out the wrinkles in your hat.

INDEX

Bewitching Breakfast in Bed / 38
Birthdays / 34, 38
Breakfast / 38
Brews & Potions / 19

Chicken Cones / 28
Chocolate Shivers / 20
Christmas / 44
Cinnamon Toast / 39
Creamy Crunchies / 16
Cucumber Christmas Tree / 44

Father's Day / 38
Frosted Funnies / 14

Ghost Floats / 22
Ghost Toast / 18
Grape Lemonaches / 21

Halloween / 40
Halloween Scream Party / 40
Hat / 45
Holidays / 33

The Little Witch's Code / 8
Lunches / 25

Mother's Day / 38

Pickled Peanut Butter Burgers / 31

Secret Spell Birthday Cake / 34
Snacks / 13
Special Occasions / 33
Spooky Sprinkle Dip / 42
Sweetheart Sandwiches / 36

Tangerine Dream Salad / 26
Ticklish Tea / 37

Utensils / 10

Valentine's Day / 36, 37
Valentine Tea Party / 36

Witch Mix-Up / 43